W9-AOX-784

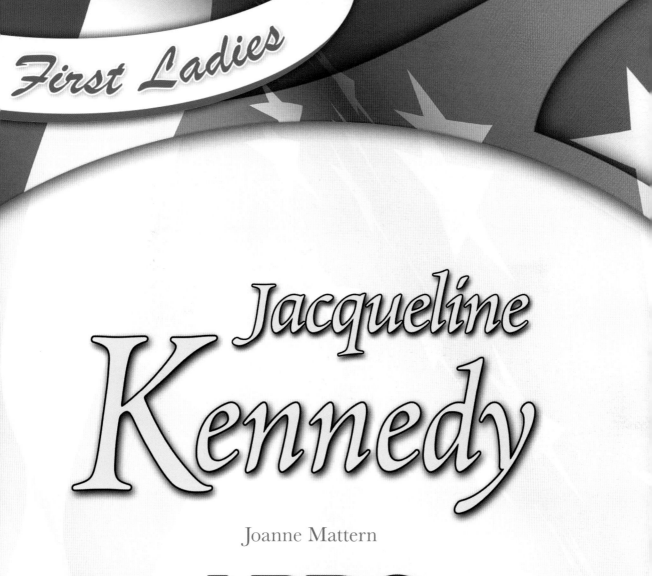

First Ladies

Jacqueline Kennedy

Joanne Mattern

ABDO
Publishing Company

visit us at
www.abdopublishing.com

Published by ABDO Publishing Company, 8000 West 78th Street, Edina, Minnesota 55439.
Copyright © 2008 by Abdo Consulting Group, Inc. International copyrights reserved in all
countries. No part of this book may be reproduced in any form without written permission from
the publisher. The Checkerboard Library™ is a trademark and logo of ABDO Publishing
Company.

Printed in the United States.

Cover Photo: Corbis
Interior Photos: AP Images p. 22; Corbis pp. 6, 13, 14, 15, 16, 20, 23, 24, 25, 27; Getty Images
    pp. 5, 17, 19, 21, 23, 26, 31; John F. Kennedy Presidential Library pp. 9, 11; John F.
    Kennedy Presidential Library (David Berne) p. 7

Series Coordinator: BreAnn Rumsch
Editors: Rochelle Baltzer, BreAnn Rumsch
Art Direction & Cover Design: Neil Klinepier

Library of Congress Cataloging-in-Publication Data

Mattern, Joanne, 1963-
  Jacqueline Kennedy / Joanne Mattern.
      p. cm. -- (First ladies)
  Includes index.
  ISBN 978-1-59928-796-6
  1. Onassis, Jacqueline Kennedy, 1929-1994--Juvenile literature. 2. Presidents' spouses--United
States--Biography--Juvenile literature. 3. Celebrities--United States--Biography--Juvenile
literature. 4. Kennedy, John F. (John Fitzgerald), 1917-1963--Juvenile literature. I. Title.

  E843.K4M38 2008
  973.922092--dc22
  [B]
                                                                          2007009730

Contents

Jacqueline Kennedy

Jacqueline Kennedy was a very popular First Lady. She was pretty and stylish, too. Everyone called her Jackie. Her husband John Fitzgerald Kennedy was the thirty-fifth president of the United States. Americans enjoyed seeing a young, lively couple leading the country.

During her time in the White House, Mrs. Kennedy made several special contributions to society. However, she was not First Lady for very long. Tragically, President Kennedy was **assassinated** after only three years in office. Americans admired Mrs. Kennedy's bravery during this difficult time.

After she left the White House, Mrs. Kennedy continued to lead a dynamic life. She was a celebrity around the world. But, she always put her family first. Mrs. Kennedy wanted her children to have normal lives away from the spotlight. For many reasons, Jacqueline Kennedy was one of America's most fascinating First Ladies.

Jacqueline Kennedy's natural grace and style made her an American icon and a popular First Lady.

Broken Family

Jacqueline Lee Bouvier was born on July 28, 1929, in Southampton, New York. Her parents, Janet and Jack Bouvier, called her Jackie. In 1933, they had a second daughter, Caroline Lee. She was called Lee.

Both of Jackie's parents came from wealthy, prominent families. When Jackie was a child, Jack ran a business on **Wall Street**. Janet managed the family's apartment in New York City, New York. Sadly, Jack and Janet did not get along well.

In 1936, the couple separated. Jackie and Lee saw their father every weekend. Jack spoiled the girls and treated them like princesses. Jackie adored him. Janet was very different. She was **strict** and made many rules for her daughters.

Jackie and her parents often attended horse shows on Long Island, New York. Jackie began riding when she was just four years old.

Janet was determined to be successful. And, she wanted the same for her daughters. Janet taught the girls how to ride horses. If Jackie fell off, Janet made sure she got right back on. Soon, Jackie was winning many prizes at horse shows.

When Jackie was 11 years old, her parents divorced. Jackie was very upset about her family's situation. She became quiet and shy. Jackie spent most of her time alone, reading books.

Jackie had many pets during her childhood, including several dogs and a bunny.

A Star at School

Despite her parents' divorce, Jackie's childhood was full of privilege. She took ballet and piano lessons. Her parents took her to art museums, and she ate in fancy restaurants.

Like other children from wealthy families, Jackie was educated in private schools. She attended the Chapin School for Girls in New York City. Jackie liked school and asked her teachers many questions. Chapin's head of school said that Jackie was one of the school's most curious students.

Sometimes Jackie's curiosity got her into trouble. She often acted up or spoke out of turn. So, Jackie was often in the head of school's office being scolded for her behavior. Eventually, Jackie settled down. She earned excellent grades and was one of Chapin's best students.

Jackie enjoyed reading and writing poetry. When she was young, she wrote a beautiful poem about walking alone on a beach. It was called "Sea Joy." Jackie never minded being alone. It gave her time to think and to dream about the future.

Jackie outside of the Chapin School for Girls on East End Avenue in New York City

A New Family

When Jackie was 13, her mother married a man named Hugh Auchincloss. Jackie's new stepfather was very wealthy. The family moved into his estate in McLean, Virginia. Their new home was called Merrywood.

Jackie and Lee were fond of their stepfather. They called him Uncle Hughdie. Hugh had been married before and already had three children. Jackie was now part of a big family. She loved living at Merrywood. But, she did not spend much time there.

When Jackie was 15, she moved to Connecticut to attend boarding school. At that time, children from wealthy families often went away to boarding schools. Jackie's new school was called Miss Porter's School for Girls. Jackie liked Miss Porter's. She earned good grades and made many friends.

Jackie wrote articles for the school newspaper. She also brought one of her horses to school and rode nearby. On weekends, she and her friends went to dances with boys from other boarding schools. Jackie enjoyed a comfortable, carefree life.

Jackie (top left) *liked her new family. She and her stepbrother Yusha* (top right) *became especially good friends.*

College and Paris

Jackie graduated from Miss Porter's in 1947. Then she attended Vassar College in Poughkeepsie, New York. At that time, Vassar was an all-girls school. Most of the school's students came from wealthy families.

Jackie studied art history and literature at Vassar. During her third year, she studied abroad at the Sorbonne, a university in Paris, France. Jackie loved living in the city and learning about French **culture**. She stayed in France for one year. During that time, Jackie also visited several other European countries.

When Jackie returned to the United States in 1950, Vassar seemed too quiet. So, she finished college at George Washington University in Washington, D.C. After she graduated in 1951, Jackie wanted to work as a **journalist**. Soon, she began her first job at the *Washington Times-Herald* newspaper.

The following year, Jackie went to a dinner party at a friend's house. One of the guests was a congressman from Massachusetts

At the Washington Times-Herald, *Jackie wrote a column called "Inquiring Camera Girl." Her job was to ask people on the street interesting questions and take their photographs.*

named John Kennedy. Later that year, John was elected to the U.S. Senate. John and Jackie got along well and enjoyed many of the same things. They began spending much of their time together.

Young Wife

In 1953, John asked Jackie to marry him. Their wedding took place on September 12. The newspapers called the event "the wedding of the year."

The **newlyweds** wanted to have children right away. However, John soon faced serious back surgery. He had to stay in bed for weeks. Yet, the couple still hoped for a family. After a few years, their dream finally came true. On November 27, 1957, their daughter, Caroline Bouvier, was born.

More than 1,200 guests attended Jackie and John's wedding reception!

John ran for the Senate again in 1958. Jackie was very busy with her husband's campaign. She went to meetings and rallies with him. She spoke to crowds of people, and everyone loved her. With Jackie's help, John easily won reelection.

John enjoyed being a senator. But he had a bigger goal in mind.
John decided to run for president of the United States. Once again,
Jackie worked hard on his campaign. She made public
appearances, gave speeches, and wrote a newspaper column.

*Jackie loved being a mother. She once said that if you don't do a good job of being
a mother, "I don't think whatever else you do well matters very much."*

First Lady

In 1960, Mr. Kennedy was the youngest U.S. president ever elected. So, the Kennedys made a big impression during the presidential inauguration.

In November 1960, John F. Kennedy was elected the thirty-fifth president of the United States. Then on November 25, a son was born to Mr. and Mrs. Kennedy. They named him John Fitzgerald Jr.

The young family moved into the White House in January 1961. But Mrs. Kennedy felt disappointed. She thought the building was run-down and uninteresting. Soon, the First Lady developed a plan to make the White House more beautiful.

First, Mrs. Kennedy made sure the White House was comfortable for her children. She turned one room into a classroom. There, she started a nursery school for Caroline as well as Caroline's cousins and friends. She also had a playground built. Soon, the White House was filled with the sounds of happy children.

The First Lady also wanted to restore the appearance of the White House to reflect America's history. She spent weeks talking to historians and artists. She found furniture and paintings that had been used by previous presidents. Slowly, the White House began to reflect the national treasure it is.

A White House Project

Mrs. Kennedy's interest in restoring the White House was about more than making a pretty home. She was committed to preserving the building's history. As a museum, the White House could represent many presidential terms. She also wanted to show Americans that their country was appealing and cultured.

In 1961, the First Lady established the Fine Arts Committee. This group aided Mrs. Kennedy in locating the important pieces of furniture that would be displayed in the White House. Later that year, the White House Historical Association was established. This group wrote a guidebook about the White House. Mrs. Kennedy wanted information about the building's history to be available to the public. The book's sales helped pay for the restoration.

In 1962, the First Lady invited television cameras inside the White House. She was the first person ever to lead a televised tour of the building. On February 14, Americans watched Mrs. Kennedy present the beautifully restored rooms. Her television program was a huge success. More than 60 million people watched it! She even won an Emmy Award for the show. Mrs. Kennedy's restoration project showed Americans they should be proud of their country's history.

A Different Style

Until the 1960s, First Ladies often stayed in the background. But Mrs. Kennedy was different. She was young and had a variety of interests. She did not want to change these parts of herself just because she was the First Lady.

Mrs. Kennedy always wore very fashionable clothes. At that time, most high-fashion clothes were made in Europe. However, the First Lady decided to promote American designers. Women everywhere loved her new look. They copied Mrs. Kennedy's style, from her clothes to her hair.

Mrs. Kennedy brought style to Washington, D.C., too. The First Lady and the president hosted elegant dinner parties for people from around the world. They also traveled to many countries together. Mrs. Kennedy loved learning about other **cultures**. And, she fascinated people everywhere she went. Many people called her "the American queen."

Mrs. Kennedy wanted the White House to become a **cultural** center for Americans. So, she invited the world's best musicians and actors to perform there. And, the Kennedys hosted parties for scientists and other important people. The First Lady's new ideas were very popular.

The Look of Camelot

Several First Ladies have been noted for their fashionable appearance. But, none have ever had such an influence on American culture as Mrs. Kennedy. After her husband was elected president, Mrs. Kennedy hired American fashion designer Oleg Cassini to create all of her clothing. Eventually, this look became known as "the Jackie look." And, women around the world wanted to copy her style.

Cassini designed every dress, jacket, and suit Mrs. Kennedy wore while she was First Lady. The fashions she preferred often featured wide, open necklines, large buttons, and simple bows. At balls and important dinners, she often wore long, white gloves to add elegance to her look. Mrs. Kennedy was also known for her pillbox hats. These box- or oval-shaped hats became very fashionable in the 1960s.

When the president and First Lady traveled to foreign countries, Mrs. Kennedy had Cassini design clothes that would complement the country's culture. This helped the Kennedys fit in better. And, it showed foreign officials that Americans understood other cultures. During this time, Americans began referring to the Kennedy presidency as "Camelot." As time passed, more people admired the Kennedys. They were soon considered American royalty.

Tragedy in Dallas

The president and First Lady were enjoying the crowds just moments before the shooting.

In 1963, President Kennedy decided to run for office again. He asked his wife to come with him on his campaign. On November 22, the Kennedys arrived in Dallas, Texas. Crowds of people cheered as they rode through the streets in an open car.

Suddenly, gunshots rang out. The president had been shot! Mrs. Kennedy held on to her husband as the car rushed to a hospital. But the doctors could not save him. Early that afternoon, John F. Kennedy died. Later, a man named Lee Harvey Oswald was arrested for President Kennedy's **assassination**.

Mrs. Kennedy was stunned and sad. She knew the American people felt the same way. Yet, she wanted to be strong for her country. Within hours of the shooting, Mrs. Kennedy stood by Vice President Lyndon Johnson as he became the new president. Then, she helped plan her husband's funeral.

The funeral was held two days later. Americans watched the ceremony on television. They mourned with Mrs. Kennedy and her children. It was one of the saddest days in American history.

Mrs. Kennedy was comforted by her children throughout her husband's funeral.

A New Home

After her husband died, Mrs. Kennedy worried about her children. Eventually, the family moved to New York City. Mrs. Kennedy loved the city. She did not feel like a celebrity there. She and her children could lead a quiet life.

However, tragedy struck the family again in June 1968. President Kennedy's brother Robert was **assassinated** after giving a speech. Mrs. Kennedy was very upset and worried about her children's safety. So, she decided it was best to leave America. Soon, her friend Aristotle Onassis asked her to marry him. Mr. Onassis was a wealthy man who lived in Greece.

On October 20, they were married. Now, Mrs. Kennedy Onassis and her children spent part of the year in Greece. They spent the rest of their time in New York City. Some Americans were upset when she remarried. They felt she had abandoned her country.

Mrs. Kennedy Onassis wanted to secure her children's future. Her second marriage gave them a safe home and a chance to see the world.

Unfortunately, the marriage did not last long. In 1975, Mr. Onassis died of a heart attack. So, Mrs. Kennedy Onassis and her children returned to New York City for good. There, she began working as an editor for a book publisher. She worked hard and knew what made a good book.

Mrs. Kennedy Onassis and her children enjoyed quiet afternoons in New York's Central Park, away from politics and reporters.

New York Landmarks

Many of Mrs. Kennedy Onassis's happiest moments were spent horseback riding with her children.

Nothing was more important to Mrs. Kennedy Onassis than her children. She worked hard to be a good mother. She made sure Caroline and John did well in school. And, she took them on trips. Mrs. Kennedy Onassis also taught them how to ride horses and enjoy many different sports. But, she did not want to spoil her children. She was proud when Caroline and John grew up to be happy, successful adults.

Mrs. Kennedy Onassis had always loved history. She felt it was important to preserve the past. So, she helped save several historic buildings in New York City. She rescued St. Bartholomew's Church and the New York Coliseum from being torn down. Later, Mrs. Kennedy Onassis helped raise money to save one of New York's most important **landmarks**, Grand Central Station.

Thanks to Mrs. Kennedy Onassis's dedication to restore Grand Central Station, thousands of people can walk through the building every day.

Mrs. Kennedy Onassis also wanted to preserve the memory of John Kennedy for her children and all Americans. She helped raise money for a presidential library in his honor. The John F. Kennedy Presidential Library and Museum opened to the public on October 21, 1979, at Columbia Point in Massachusetts.

Last Years

Mrs. Kennedy Onassis continued to live and work in New York City for the rest of her life. Her good friend Maurice Tempelsman kept her company. She also spent time with Caroline and John. In addition, Mrs. Kennedy Onassis enjoyed being a grandmother to Caroline's three children. The family enjoyed summers together at a beach home on Martha's Vineyard in Massachusetts.

In 1994, Mrs. Kennedy Onassis became sick with **cancer**. Her doctors thought she should stay in the hospital. But, she wanted to be at home with her family and friends.

Mrs. Kennedy Onassis and Maurice Tempelsman visit in Central Park.

On May 19, 1994, Mrs. Kennedy Onassis died in her New York apartment. She was buried next to John F. Kennedy at Arlington National Cemetery in Virginia.

Mrs. Kennedy Onassis led an extraordinary life. She was a privileged child, a newspaper photographer, a wife, a mother, a First Lady, a book editor, and a social figure. She faced these roles with style and grace. Today, Jacqueline Kennedy remains one of America's most celebrated First Ladies.

Throughout her life, Jacqueline Kennedy maintained her privacy. Yet, she was an inspiration to many people.

Timeline

1929	Jacqueline Lee Bouvier was born on July 28.
1944–1947	Jackie attended Miss Porter's School for Girls.
1947–1950	Jackie attended Vassar College; she spent her third year in France, studying at the Sorbonne.
1950–1951	Jackie finished college at George Washington University.
1951	Jackie began working at the *Washington Times-Herald*.
1953	Jackie married John F. Kennedy on September 12.
1957	The Kennedys' daughter, Caroline, was born on November 27.
1960	The Kennedys' son, John Jr., was born on November 25.
1961–1963	Mrs. Kennedy acted as First Lady, while Mr. Kennedy served as president.
1963	President Kennedy was assassinated on November 22.
1968	Robert F. Kennedy was assassinated in June; Mrs. Kennedy married Aristotle Onassis on October 20.
1975	Mr. Onassis died of a heart attack; Mrs. Kennedy Onassis began working as an editor in New York City, New York.
1979	The John F. Kennedy Presidential Library and Museum opened on October 21.
1994	Mrs. Kennedy Onassis died on May 19.

Did You Know?

As a young girl, some of Jackie's favorite books were *The Jungle Book*, *Robin Hood*, and *Gone with the Wind*.

In 1950, Jackie won a *Vogue* magazine writing contest with her essay titled "People I Wish I Had Known." Due to her parents' wishes, she turned down the prize of a yearlong training position at the magazine.

During her husband's presidential campaign, Mrs. Kennedy wrote a newspaper column called "The Candidate's Wife."

At 31, Mrs. Kennedy was the third-youngest First Lady. And, she was the first First Lady to bring a baby into the White House in 100 years.

Mrs. Kennedy was the first First Lady to employ a press secretary. She was also the first president's wife to appear on the cover of a magazine.

Mrs. Kennedy could speak several foreign languages, including French, Spanish, and Italian.

Mrs. Kennedy traveled more than any previous First Lady. She visited many countries, including France, England, Morocco, India, Greece, Italy, Venezuela, and Pakistan.

Glossary

assassinate - to murder a very important person, usually for political reasons.

cancer - any of a group of often deadly diseases characterized by an abnormal growth of cells that destroys healthy tissues and organs.

culture - the customs, arts, and tools of a nation or people at a certain time.

journalist - a person who collects and edits news for presentation to the public.

landmark - an important structure of historical or physical interest.

newlywed - a person who just married.

strict - demanding others to follow rules or regulations in a rigid, exact manner.

Wall Street - a U.S. financial center in New York City, New York, that includes the site of the New York Stock Exchange.

Web Sites

To learn more about Jacqueline Kennedy, visit ABDO Publishing Company on the World Wide Web at **www.abdopublishing.com**. Web sites about Jacqueline Kennedy are featured on our Book Links page. These links are routinely monitored and updated to provide the most current information available.

Index